OLDETIME FEATS OF STRENGTH

FORGOTTEN STRENGTH

★ 101 ★

JOHN "THE VIKING" MOUSER

Copyright Pending 2018

All rights reserved. No part of this publication may be reproduced, distributed or transmitted in any form or by any means, including photocopying, recording, or other electronic or mechanical methods, without the prior written permission of the publisher, except in the case of brief quotations embodied in critical reviews and certain other noncommercial uses permitted by copyright law.

Foreward

Ye Oldey Timey Strength

By Cedric Nye

For a long time, people have looked at the Strongmen and Strongwomen among us, and been in awe of the seemingly effortless way in which they perform incredible feats of strength. History is rife with stories of people who had exceptional strength: From Samson toppling the pillars to Hercules doing all those Hercules-type things, and many, many more. The average person gazes upon these acts with awe, and will never forget what they've seen- but the few of you who have the urge, the calling- gaze upon those feats of strength, and want more than anything to have that strength for yourself.

Well, now is your chance to learn how to do some of those feats. John Mouser will introduce you to three exciting feats of strength: How to tear a deck of cards, how to bend a horseshoe, and how to drive a nail through solid wood with your hand. Time to choose whether you will read history, or be a part of history. Welcome to the world of the Strongman!

Table Of Contents

Chapter One: Card Tearing 1

    List of Playing Cards and their Difficulty

Chapter Two: Horseshoe Bending 9

    Anatomy of the Horseshoe

    List of Horseshoes and their Difficulty

Chapter Three: Human Hammer 21

Chapter One: Card Tearing

Below is a list of playing cards. They are listed in order from least difficult to most difficult.

1. Cheap paper cards. These are not coated.
2. The Dollar Tree 2 pack
3. Aviators
4. Hoyle
5. Mavericks
6. Bicycles
7. Actual casino cards

I recommend starting off with the cheap paper cards (if you can find them) or the Dollar Tree 2 pack. Start off with about 5-10 cards at a time. Once you can easily tear those, add 2-5 cards to the stack. Once you can tear an entire deck, move on to the next deck on the list. You may need to start out with less than a full deck when you attempt a more difficult deck.

Place the cards in your Non-Dominant (ND) hand. Adjust the deck so that you are holding it near the bottom with just your index finger, middle finger and thumb.

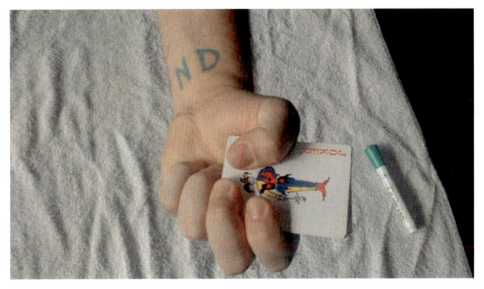

Grip the deck fairly tight without bowing the deck inwards. Turn your ND hand over so that your knuckles are facing up and the deck faces the floor.

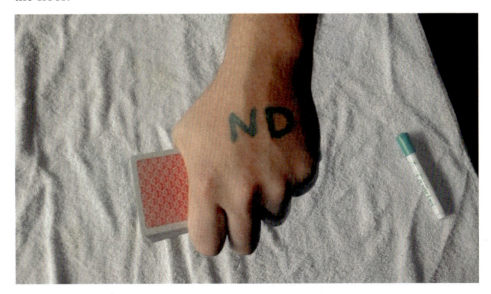

Grab the exposed part of the deck with your Dominant (D) hand. Your thumb should be on top of the deck. The tip of your thumb of your D hand should be lightly pressed against the side of the ND hand near (slightly distal) the base knuckle. The rest of the D hand should be under the deck.

The middle knuckle of the index finger should be directly underneath where the thumb is. You should be squeezing the thumb and knuckle of the index finger together on the D hand. This should be similar to how you would squeeze the bottle cap on a small soda when opening it. The next step is the most difficult to learn. But once you figure it out, you'll never lose it! Keeping both hands in position you are going to use the tip of the index finger on your ND hand and middle knuckle of the index finger on your D hand to slightly move the cards and make them very rigid.

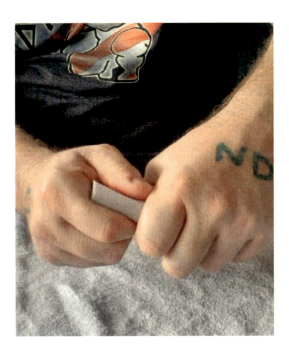

The cards should feel stiff right in the middle near the index finger of the D hand. This is somewhat similar to holding out a sheet of paper without letting it droop. Although a different technique is used, the idea is the same. Once the cards are rigid you are ready to begin tearing. Make sure you are squeezing tightly with both hands. Start to pronate your D hand. This should be a similar motion to turning OFF the ignition key in your vehicle. If you need to, think about taking the middle knuckle of your D hand and moving it along the outside of the ND hand. As you're doing this, very, very slightly curl the wrist of your ND hand towards the floor.

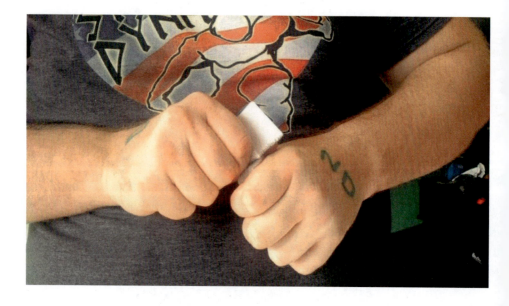

Once the deck begins to tear, keep pronating the D hand until it seems that you cannot go any further and the deck has stopped tearing. Once the tear has stopped, you'll need to slightly adjust the D hand. Move the D hand (but maintain the same hand position) down so that your thumb and middle knuckle of your index finger are closer to where the tear has stopped.

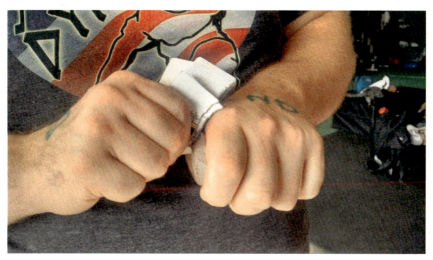

Pinch down firmly and pronate again, tearing the deck just like before. Don't forget to curl the wrist of the ND hand ever so slightly. Continue this procedure until you have torn the deck completely in half.

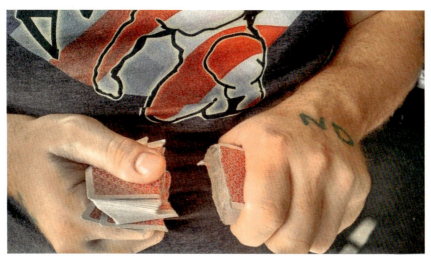

Chapter Two: Horseshoe Bending

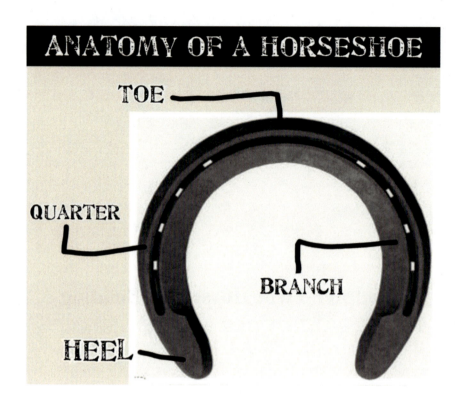

Not all horseshoes are created equal. Below is a Horseshoe Progression where the horseshoes are listed from easiest to most difficult to bend. There are dozens of different types and brands of horseshoe. I listed the easiest ones to get started on. Once you've successfully bent all the horseshoes on this list it will be time to start experimenting further!

Horseshoe Progression:

1. Thoro 'Bred Racing Plate Lite Training Size 6 FR TB
2. St. Croix Forge Ultralite #2
3. St. Croix Forge Ultralite #1
4. St. Croix Forge Polo #2
5. Diamond Front Competitor 2FBDC
6. St. Croix Forge Polo #1

You'll need a horseshoe and 3 leather or suede wraps for this. Take the horseshoe in your dominant (D) hand. Hold the horseshoe out in front of you so that it looks like a "C" (from your perspective) if you're left handed or a backwards "C" (from your perspective) if you're right handed.

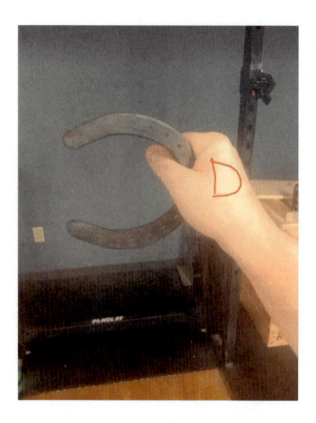

While holding it out in this position you'll want to wrap the quarters and branches. Each branch/quarter will be wrapped with leather or suede starting on the side of the horseshoe that is facing you.

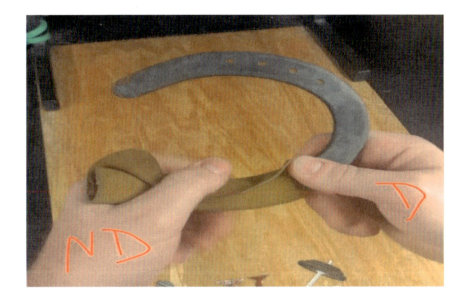

The leather will be hanging down, then wrapped towards the side facing away from you and up.

Wrap as tightly as you can. Continue wrapping until all the leather is tightly around the branch/quarter. Then wrap the other branch/quarter the exact same way.

Now bring the horseshoe back out in front of you in the starting position.

It should look like a "C" or a backwards "C" depending on which hand is dominant. Your D hand should grip the bottom branch clear up onto the heel. Your palm should be facing down.

Your non-dominant (ND) hand should now grip the upper quarter clear up near the heel. The ND hand should also be palm down.

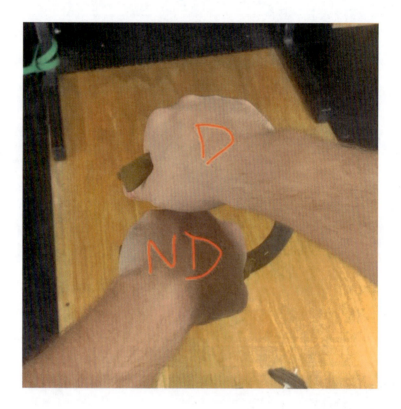

Start tightening the suede with your hands over the wraps just as they are. You'll want to do this until the leather stops moving. The tighter the wraps, the easier the bend will be.

Once the wraps are tight, move the horseshoe to the side of your hip/upper leg. You'll need to turn your torso in that direction in order to get in the correct position.

If you are right-handed you'll go to the left hip. If you are left handed you'll go to the right hip. The toe of the horseshoe should be braced on your hip/upper thigh. You will probably want to put a piece of leather under the toe of the shoe to keep from beating up your leg until you get used to it. If you've done this correctly the thumb of your D hand should be away from your body and the thumb of your ND hand should be near your body.

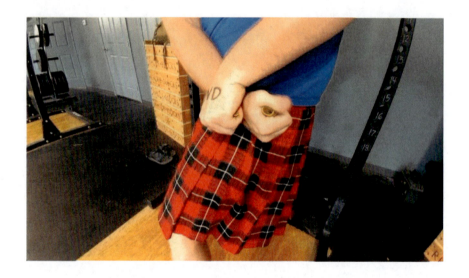

Begin pulling with your D hand. Most of this pull should be initiated by your lat and by rotating your trunk away from the horseshoe. Simultaneously, you should be pushing with your ND hand. The higher up on the heel of the horseshoe you can get, the easier this will be.

Bend the horseshoe as far as you can this way. Once you've exhausted the limits of this technique and the horseshoe is straightened out a bit, you'll switch to a different position. Take and place the horseshoe on your thigh or hip. It doesn't matter which leg, just whichever one you feel stronger on. You want the center (toe) of the horseshoe on your thigh/hip and the heels pointed up and away from you find a spot on your hip or thigh where you have a really good fulcrum.

You may want to place a piece of leather or suede under the horseshoe. Your left hand should grab the left branch/quarter near the heel and your right hand should grab the right branch/quarter near the heel. With arms straight (nearly locked out) you want to bear down on the horseshoe with all your weight and press with your arms.

You may naturally start to drop into a kind of lunge. Keep bearing down and pressing until the horseshoe is straight!!

Chapter Three: Human Hammer

For this feat you'll need a 1" thick pine board, a nail, a piece of leather or suede, a claw hammer, 2 folding chairs and a writing utensil. The board should be 12"x24". The board will need to be placed across 2 surfaces with a space in the middle. 2 folding chairs work great. Folding chairs are usually the perfect height. Set the chairs facing away from one another and place the board on the back of the chairs at the highest point.

There should be ~12" of space between the chairs. It is important to note that the chairs need to be standing on a solid surface with no give or rebound. Now that the board is ready, you'll need to prepare the nail, your hand and your position. First, prepare the leather then grab the nail. This should be a 10-16d nail. Later on you can experiment with larger nails, but stick with 10-16d for now. **DO NOT** attempt this feat **WITHOUT** the leather. Suede strips of 3"x6" or 4"x8" works great. Start folding 1 end of the leather over. Use 1" folds. Leave about 2" unfolded at the end.

Place the suede into the palm of your Dominant (D) hand. The unfolded portion should be near your fingers, not your wrist. Make sure the leather is centered with your hand. Now place the head of the nail into the center of the leather.

This should also be centered in the palm and right at the base of the fingers. Close your hand into a fist allowing the nail to protrude out from between the middle and ring fingers. You can use the unfolded portion of the suede to pull up around the nail so that the nail is not in direct contact with the ring or middle fingers.

Now to get into position. Stand between the chairs with the board in front of you. With the nail and leather in your D hand, place the point of the nail on the center of the board.

While holding the nail in the center of the board, slowly walk backwards until your arm is straight and you're slightly bent forward. Your feet should be even with each other at this point.

Take 1 step forward with the foot opposite the D hand.

Take 1 step backwards with the foot on the same side as the D hand. Your back foot should **NOT** be directly behind the lead foot.

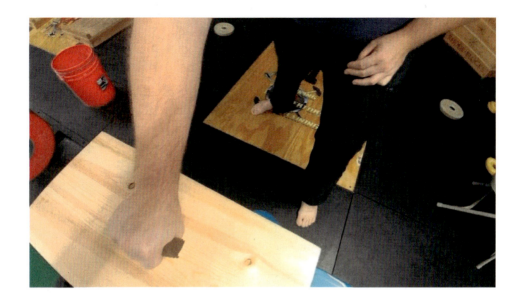

Your hips should be facing the board. The lead foot and rear foot should be rather wide. Don't be afraid to make minor adjustments in the stance. While maintaining your stance and keeping the nail in the middle of the board, you'll need to slightly adjust your hand so that it is in the ideal position for when it impacts the board. The ideal position is where the nail is perfectly straight up and down.

Your wrist may not be perfectly straight for this to happen. Now it's time to swing the hammer! I'm going to describe the swing to you in this paragraph. I recommend that before each attempt, you should go through the motions very slowly and precisely. You want to make sure that you're going to hit the board where you want to. You will also want to make sure that you are going to impact the board with the nail being completely vertical. While maintaining your stance and keeping the nail in position in your hand, you will draw your arm (D hand) back behind you and swing it in a semi circle up over your head.

Your arm should remain straight during the entire swing. The swing should be very controlled and should get faster as you go.

Once your arm is overhead and beginning its descent towards the board, you will need to put all of your force into the swing.

Just as the nail is about to make contact with the wood, you need to lean forward slightly while simultaneously dropping your bodyweight some. Let your knees bend and allow your bodyweight to help you drive the nail. Do this without pushing your arm forward. Your arm may bend slightly here.

Once you've impacted the board you'll want to check and see if the nail went completely through the board.

Use a claw hammer to remove the nail before you try again. **DO NOT** drive in another nail until you've removed the last one. Draw a tight circle around the hole where the nail was.

This lets you know if you accidentally punch through the same hole later. Once there are alot of holes in the board, you'll want to get a new one.

Made in the USA
Columbia, SC
11 April 2019